Poetry from the
Heart

To Sister Teresa,

Thank you very much for your sisterhood, support and fun times at the casinos.

Sister Regina Long Smithhill

February 3, 2007

Poetry from the Heart

Regina Long Southall

To order additional copies of this book, contact:
Xlibris Corporation
1-888-795-4274
www.Xlibris.com
Orders@Xlibris.com
35521

Contents

Dedication

This book of poems is dedicated to three women in my life, who inspired me to continue to strive for success. Even if it means encountering long, hard, tiring hours of struggle, keep going. These women are my mother, Leslie Crocker Long; my grandmother, Corine "Moody" Wright; and my great-aunt, Anne Martin. It was because of their efforts and continuous reinforcement that allowed me to be where I am today. To God and them, I give thanks and honor. They knew I would stick with the task until it was tackled to the end. They also knew I never gave up without a fight. Thanks, Mama, Moody, and Aunt Anne.

INTRODUCTION

It has always been important to me to let the world know about my capabilities. I have become a teacher, speaker, and writer. I express the way I feel about issues through writing. This practice of literary composition allows me to vent depression, anxiety, loneliness, and failure. I have always dreamed to become a writer as early as my youth.

Participating in writing contests allowed me one way to express myself.

I have had a rich life that involved many true-to-life experiences. I have always had the opportunity to travel with my great-aunt, as early as age six. I would go to New Jersey the day school closed for summer vacation. I would stay until Labor Day. During this time, I was able to travel to many places and see what many children only read about. I have a rich legacy of time well spent, learning about the wonders of the world. I will never forget going to Cape Cod, Massachusetts, touring the area where President John F. Kennedy stayed for summer relaxation. I also had an opportunity to go to the Plymouth Rock and see firsthand where the Pilgrims landed in America in 1620. My great-aunt would always remind me that all of her vacation photos always included me.

When life ends for me, I can truly say I have lived a full life. I have seen a lot. Sometimes obstacles got in the way, but I always managed to overcome each time. Having faith and guidance from God, I have endured. I have grown through experiences. What I have seen or done has made me a stronger individual. People have tried to pull me down sometimes, but I would press on.

People that I thought were my friends sometimes misunderstood my point of view. They had to always be right. In the final analysis, they were not true friends anyway.

I am retired now and have time to expand everything I desire to accomplish. This book of poetry I have written can help you reach your goals. When you take the time to read my collection of poetry, you will find life worth living. You too will reach for the stars without hesitation.

The Neighbors We Should Be

It was a quiet Thursday morning in September,
When hurricane Isabel came rushing by.
Her wind was strong and gusty, as trees began to fly.
So many were without power, and food began to spoil.
We asked ourselves how we managed without even a kerosene lamp of oil.
Some even lost everything that was so dear.
But God was in control, and there was no need to fear.
Many lives have been changed, and there is a reason to pause, to stop and think how important we are to each other one and all.
We had to come together and help out where we could.
Sometimes it takes a period of crisis for man to realize the importance of brotherhood.
God destroyed material things and helped us to see,
a pot of coffee, an extension cord, and the removal of a tree, made us the neighbors we should be.

Another Day

Relax and enjoy another day.
Don't let time get in the way.
Things change so very fast,
You'll never know what moment will be your last.
Sit back and reflect upon a moment of peace.
Before you know it, that moment will cease.
While you have a chance, think about how good life has been.
Battles occur along the way.
Just think of those you did win.
I have been successful through struggles, my friend.
Enduring makes a stronger person of us, moving on without a fuss.
As circumstances arise and life continues . . . pray.
                          Relax and enjoy another day.

The Life I've Lived

God has granted me a chance to live, having been born a premature child; only He knew what I had to give.
I achieved many goals I set out to do, becoming a teacher, speaker, and writer, just to name a few.
I'm thankful for the time I had a chance to show the world that this once pillow-size baby had goals to acquire.
Many were met before I decided to retire.
A mother, grandmother, and great-aunt always giving encouragement caused me to never give up on any task placed before me.
Today has made me appreciate accomplishments mankind would never vividly see.
The life I've lived has been good, and my tomorrows will continue to produce great things.
It's so nice to accept what life brings.

A Job Well Done

I often sit reflecting upon my dreams.
Wondering why there is an obstacle here, it seems.
Trying to accomplish what I set out to do,
What's preventing my dreams from coming true?
Wanting to be a children's book writer has not come to pass.
Can't anyone see what I do is a blast?
I've worried, struggled, and stressed myself out,
Having to participate at a convention in order to tout.
Life is a chance I have to take, but my writing tends to be in the wake.
I have more days behind then ahead.
Give me a chance to capture my dreams and see that I've
won, enriching lives to come.
When I'm gone, others will be reminded of a job well done.

My Poetry Will Burn

As the sun is rising
I always think of me,
Knowing what I want to be.
I can write verses that may be long.
When my goal has been reached,
I will have accomplished what I have taught.
I yearn to do my best, and I know all of my poetry will burn.

Becoming a Poet

As I look out into the horizon,
Nothing looks familiar to me.
But I know I'll reach my journey being free.
As I become the poet I desire to be.

The Effects of Hurricane Katrina on Our Nation

Hurricane Katrina destroyed so many places.
This disaster has left a lump in my throat.
August 29, 2005, brought strain to many faces.
People were not able to get to safety, not even in a boat.

Michael Brown is director of FEMA and Michael Chertoff, secretary of homeland securities,
Were the two Michaels really doing a good job?
They have made so many people sob.
Each Michael covers for the other.
That's because black "folks" aren't their true brothers.
They continue to say not to dwell on what has happened, but to move forward.
How can you go on if government officials are lacking across the board?
Looking at the city of New Orleans, there are now no more means.
So many have died because they didn't have a chance, and no true way to advance.
Our president falls in that group of leaders who took their time while so many people
became defeaters.

What is the world coming to? Honest politicians are so few.
Now that thousands have lost their lives, leaders are now trying to hide behind the jive.
People across the nation can clearly see, unfair treatment was meant to be.
They always find money for what they wish to do, but now in a tragedy of this magnitude,
having all reasons for not moving quickly,
Michael and Michael continue to elude.

Some eighty days when they say the water will be gone,
Families of the dead will have nothing left but a missing link in their close bond.
How quickly we were able to send soldiers to Iraq and leave others back home unprotected, in
a sense of lack.
Can you believe now that FEMA is saying to implement steps to get through this tragedy?
Why weren't steps in place when it was known that people must flee?
Now that hundreds are dead and rescue teams are doing their best, these are truly implementations
that have not passed the test.
Floodwaters are up to the rooftops one week later. People that did survive do not have a job
or home to go to.
Government officials don't have a clue. Had tragedy struck them in the same way as the ordinary
man, would their loved ones been canned?

They keep saying our capabilities are sound to move the world. Where were those capabilities when Katrina waters began to swirl? Don't keep saying we were able to rebuild after the San Francisco disaster 100 years ago. Back then facilities were very low.

You continue to say what we overcame years ago when we bring up what local, state, and federal governments lacked days ago.

Had the government sent those buses, planes, and trains, American citizens would not have suffered such a tremendous strain.

This has been such an emotional trauma for all, even those around the country that didn't even fall.

How can children involved ever forget, the things they and their loved ones endured causing such fret.

Only God can ease my pain, at my expense while dignitaries gain. They will continue to walk tall.

One day God will come to their doorsteps and make them fall. By then it will be too late to say I'm sorry for the way I treated my fellow men. There is no harmony in this land. A fist full of dollars just won't do.

It can't bring back a loved one whose life was cut short because of you. The whole universe will suffer this great loss as the government continues to blight us at a cost. Homes, jobs, and above all dignity are gone down the drain. People who have worked so hard have nothing else to gain. Lord, have mercy on my weary soul. Why have our leaders been so cold? Down the road so many stories will be told. The truth is what needs to be said. There will be no need to know what our world was about, being run by leaders with so much clout.

Who Is Going to Attend to This Mess?

My state, Virginia, was devastated by Hurricane Isabel.
Disaster has hit the nation once again.
Hurricane Katrina has left the Gulf Coast in disbelief.
Will there ever be some relief?
When an entire city is underwater, worrying about little things is certainly out of order.
As water rises higher, bodies lay dead under live wire.
Those involved were poor, middle class, and the well-to-do.
Silver and gold are in the aftermath too.
Millions of lives have been lost, and we can't estimate a cost.
Tears have been shed for those in distress.
Who is going to attend to this mess?

The Twenty-first Century

The twenty-first century has really come in with despair.
Does anyone really care?
Our troubles all started with the 911 blast.
We had hoped that would have been the last.
Then came hurricanes, Isabel, Katrina, and Rita, just to name a few.
What are we going to do?
Gas prices have soared, and we can't understand why.
What next tragedy will bring up another lie?
As days go by and the sun begins to shine,
A place to stay for some will be very hard to find.

A Gift from Above

To be able to wake up is a gift from above.
God is always with us and offering His love.
Life may be hard for me and you,
But God Almighty will see us through.
I try to be happy, but sometimes I grow sad.
Yet being alive soon makes me glad.
So many friends my age are gone.
Their names are on gravesites etched in stone.
Thank you, God, for what you have allowed me to do.
Many times I forget what I've tried to overcome, you already knew.
Guide my feet to continue to press forward, leaning on knowing you, Lord,
To be able to wake up is truly a gift from above.

I Need to Be Free

Having raised my children I need to be free.
I fed them, rocked them, and gave them love.
Watching over them, God guided me from above.
Now is the time to think about me.
Becoming of age is the time for them to go,
Living their lives now and letting me be.
I'm retired and have no job.
I won't sob if they let me be.
I need to be free.

My Best

I tried hard to do my best,
Having to always take a test.
I want to achieve what I set out to do.
However, trials always seem to get in the way.
Hopefully, my pie in the sky will come someday.

Within My Heart

Within my heart there is a place for you.
A place that stands for nothing else.
The place I hope will never be left,
But will live on from sunrise to sunset.
A place that I can cherish until the end,
When nothing else is left on earth but sin.

Within my heart you will forever stand.
I know you will, because you said I can.
While others are heartbroken and left alone,
I will always be able to hear the great tone within my heart,
Which others lose and go astray. You will never go away,
My special one today and forever that is hidden within my heart.

A Beautiful Butterfly

I saw a butterfly in my yard.
I tried to catch it, but it was very hard.
Its colors, of yellow and black, made it flutter like a jack.
Flying from bush to bush made me have to rush.
I think it knew I was trying to catch it.
As I reached for the butterfly, it flew to a higher limb.
Continuing on its way, moving so swiftly by,
I looked as it soared up in the sky.
The butterfly flew away, but just seeing it made my day.

Ode to Jordan

My daughter has a dog named Jordan.
He is my pride and joy,
He loves to play with toys.
Whenever he comes to see me,
He is as cuddly as can be.

Jordan is a pretty brown terrier,
Who could ask for a pet any merrier?
He wakes you up when he wants to play,
And when he goes outside, he wants you to stay.
He gets plenty of rest, sleeping while you are away,
Getting in his favorite spot on the bed,
He curls up until it is time to be fed.

Jordan knows specific words, like food, eat, outside, and go.
Just hearing those words will raise his ears,
But sometimes I have to say no.
He listens when you are talking to him,
Not even making a whimper.

Jordan loves for you to share meat with him.
He loves french fries and usually eats all of them.
All he needs to hear is food hitting the side of his tin dish,
He'll come running from wherever he is.
In a flash he gobbles up fritters like a fish.

Jordan knows when his master gets home.
He listens and knows the right car alarm.
He can tell which one is his master's sound.
Jordan is the smartest dog around.

Night Flight

Traveling by plane at night,
I sit quietly and write.
I think of beauty as the plane soars.
The city I'm leaving goes out of sight.
The plane glides on a cool October night.
As it moves across God's dark sky,
I gaze out the window and realize I'm up very high.
There is nothing but darkness below.
Now and then a faint light down low will glow.
I always pray that my flight will be safe,
Hoping to land smoothly as the plane approaches the runway.
I begin to see the ground as I look out.
I realize God had His long arms all around me.
Having Him riding with me, there is no reason to doubt.

Things to Remember

Sometimes we forget what others do for us.
Just saying thank you is a must.
Those little things mean so much.
Taking in the mail, putting out the trash, picking up the newspaper; just keeping in touch.
These are the things that mean a lot.
When money is gone and kindness is all we have,
It's so nice to recall what people do.
It lets you know that friendship is true.
And it's easy to recall a precious time,
It will always stay with you when years continue and you have reached your prime.

A School Year Ends

As this school year comes to an end,
We know God has been our closest friend.
He's given Portsmouth a school board, teachers, and parents who have worked hard to
help kids.
One hundred eighty days have almost passed by,
Kids have studied, played, and sometimes asked why?
We appreciate the days now behind us, and from Your guidance, we have everlasting trust.
Sometimes it's hard for our school system to agree,
But all we had to do was put out trust in Thee.
As we go forward continuing to do our best,
Let us be good role models to pass each and every test.

Reflections

As I sit on a balcony in the breezy Georgia air,
Reflecting upon my pass, the wind blows my hair.
I recall how Mama reminded me to stay close to home.
She always wanted to see me as I played with my ball alone.
I would bounce it against the stone.
Sometimes it hit the steps, making me moan
I did not know what Mama would say,
Knowing my ball may bounce another way.
Once I missed and hit the storm door,
Glass shattered all over the house floor.
I was punished for what I did,
But Mama knew I had been obedient.
She still praised me for minding her,
By staying close to home instead of going about,
Remember that unsafe streets are not a good hangout.

Anchorman Peter Jennings

I was saddened when anchorman Peter Jennings died.
He was a man who had great stride.
Peter put his heart in what he reported as world news.
He wasn't one who had to pick and choose.
Whenever I was home at half past six,
Channel 13 was where my dial was fixed.
Peter would tell you what was happening around the world.
He was another Edward R Meryl.
He loved his job, and you could tell,
He always made his news jell.

Where, Where, Where's the Teacher?

Where, where, where's the teacher?
Where can she be?
We're overloaded with so many kids; it's hard for us to see.

Kids, kids, kids everywhere, never seeing the end of the pile,
We line them up sss, then down the hall we file.

We try, try, and try real hard, to teach them all we can.
We plan and teach, teach and plan, but still need another hand.

Help, help, help, us please, we're working to the bone.
With all these kids in one classroom, we feel we're in twilight zone.

Where, where, where's the teacher? Oh where can she be?
It was said she would be coming real soon,
But soon you know it will be June.
Where, where, where's the teacher? Oh where can she be?
We're overloaded with so many kids; it's hard for us to see.

Never Give Up

When I'm sad and lonely, I must not give in.
I know there are many trials; I will not win.
I can only pray and ask God to see me through,
Knowing only he can make my life brand-new.
If I'm troubled, God is the only one I can turn to,
Embracing me and telling me I love you.

It's Your Day

Make your day a happy one and enjoy the sun.
Spend each day as you wish, eating your favorite dish.
Pamper yourself whenever you can, please you and not man.
Be good and attend to your needs.
God will reward you for all of your good deeds.

Seventy Plus Years of Service

You have given seventy plus years of service.
Christ loves you so.
He has showered you with blessings, more than you will ever know.
Living a life for Jesus has made you what you are.
Faith in Him has brought you very, very far.
Ebenezer is honored to have a member who cares the way you do.
Your love for God and people has made the world brand-new.
You have given seventy plus years of service.
Christ loves you so.
He has showered you with blessings, more than you will ever know.

Now That You Are Retired

Thank God for every day you are able to rise.
Retiring was a decision that was very wise.
Live each and every day to the fullest.
Begin to fill your life with a relish of zest.
Enjoy yourself and do all the things you never had a chance to do,
Getting to the bank and post office before it closes to name a few.
You can eat without getting indigestion.
Being at lunch more than thirty minutes will not be a
Matter to question.
You won't have to do lesson plans every Sunday night.
Just watch your favorite shows and turn off the light.
Buy what you want because you can't take anything with you when it's all said and done.
Go shopping and have some fun.
Please yourself first and then others.
In the final analysis, others don't really care anyway.
You're the one in need of the holiday.
Enjoy yourself all the time.
Don't leave anyone one thin dime.

Can't You Understand?

Why can't people understand how you feel?
The things they do always bring about ill will.
Thinking only what matters for them makes you feel like the one trying to condemn.
If only they could recognize how you are affected by what they do,
Then they would realize your point of view.
When they misinterpret what you say, lines of communication then become one way.
Understanding what is meant is the key.
Then there would be no need to disagree.

My Kind of Store

Farm Fresh at 701-A N. Battlefield Boulevard is my kind of store.
Whenever I go there, I always buy more.
Moving my cart down aisles to shelves,
I sometimes see employees working like little elves.
The layout is neat and clean.
Try shopping there, and you'll find out what I mean.

Happy Seventieth Birthday Uncle Clifton

I wish you a happy seventieth birthday, Uncle Clifton.
Today you are a real top gun.
You've always been a help to others, especially to your sister who was my dear mother.
Be thankful for all seventy years God has granted you.
Your name should be listed in Who's Who.
Relax and reflect upon how good God has been, allowing you to stay here seven times ten.
Enjoy your day and have some fun.
All we can say is well done.

32.8 Years of Teaching

I taught school for 32.8 years, starting out shedding many tears.
It was hard for a black teacher to get attention,
Most times the good things done were never mentioned.
I'd start my day teaching all the subjects I had to plan.
Many times I had to give others a helping hand.
I served as grade chairman for many years,
Getting only five extra dollars in my check every two weeks, making only one hundred dollars more for what I had to earn.
Overworking, a regular teacher is what a system seeks, knowing I could never be weak.
Times when a teacher calls in sick,
Instead of getting a substitute, the regular teacher got the short end of the stick.
Splitting up a class for the absent teacher was no fun; you'd get them, and no substitute plan was done.
As six more kids were added to your twenty, you never got a thank-you or even an extra penny.
I worked hard in everything I did, and the system cared less, even though I did more to show progress.
Only those that licked and lapped got praise.
It took me years to get a decent raise.
I took my weekends to write my plans, trying to regroup a thought. Times like this are what life brought.
Traveling out of town for some fun, to the backseat of the car I would run.
With papers, manuals, books, and class register in hand,
I would be working on demand.
I would work some six hours to get things done, not stopping until the setting of the sun.
As my husband drove into the hotel parking lot, I'd gather up my things because by this time I am hot.
My school job was never done, and I put my heart in all I did.
I worked real hard but never won, creating workshops that were a hole in one.
I earned my 32.8 years working in education.
It was truly a sensation.

Thank You, God

Thank you, God, for all you do.
I have so much to appreciate because of You.
You woke me up this morning and started me on my way, granting me another day.
You gave me a chance to see once more the things you have provided me to adore.
I don't know what I would do without You.
Blessings from you outshine anything man can do.

God Is Getting Our Attention

God is getting our attention, state by state.
People have died at an alarming rate.
There have been floods, hurricanes, and earthquakes.
Windstorms and rain have kept everyone on edge,
It seems that water continues to fill our lakes and sometimes reaches a window ledge.
He is definitely trying to tell us something, knowing that God is king.
We must stop and take note.
Time is running out for this old place and
Then we'll have to see God face-to-face.
When the chips fall, all nationalities will be in the same boat,
Trying to swim to safety by staying afloat,
There will be no time to say I'm sorry and no time to forgive or write even a love note.
When God gets our attention, we have to stop and thank Him for the time he has let us live.
To him the glory we must always give.
When this old world comes to a close,
Those not ready will be separated from those that rose.
God is getting our attention state by state.
Get yourself ready before it is too late.

A Man Named King

There once was a man who was a wonder of the world.
He loved man, woman, boy, and girl.
He wanted peace long ago, always telling the world so.
He worked for good and not for bad,
Because of this got shot and made us sad.
His name was Martin Luther King, Jr.
I only wish he could have made peace sooner.
He left behind a mark in words, deeds, and ideas for this our world to follow.
What he did make us look at our world in hope for a brighter tomorrow.

The Calm of the Day

In the calmness of the day, a cool breeze blows my way.
I sit and think about my life,
How God has brought me through much strife.
While sitting I am able to see, rewards I've obtained without a fee.
I struggled sometimes to get ahead but always managed to tread.
Many days I worked from sunup to sundown,
But I always kept my feet on solid ground.
Being persistent in all I do, what I have accomplished has vouched for time well spent,
not knowing what God in heaven has sent.
I began working when I was a teen and hung in there because working became routine.
I am at peace with myself because I know what I've done has made me glad.
I've given the world all that I had.
And when the breeze ceases to blow
And the calm of the day is no-show,
My God was in charge of all I have ever gained.
He was the One who made me sustained.

Once a Teacher

I was once a teacher in the elementary school,
Always thinking teaching was so cool.
I started when I was twenty-two
Becoming a teacher was nothing new.

Things learned in college gave me a start,
But being in the real world made the task a wee bit hard.
I always had my lesson plans.
You never knew when someone would try to catch you off guard.
Knowing they would make my job so very hard.
Those in authority got a kick out of you being unprepared, so they could get one more brownie card.

Mr. Telephone Man

Mr. Telephone Man, get Sophia on the line.
Four friends and I need to talk to her.
Don't count us out, please, dear sir.
We will be with Sophia all the way,
Standing in the rain every day.
Sophia is our earth angel of love,
Who communicates over the radio as friendly as a dove.
I know she will hit it off with me in the crew, and my friends too.
Just a little bit of love is all it takes,
To make the six of us become a keepsake.
Our partnership will last forever.
With hope, it will never sever.
Together we will be a new edition, having desirous ambition.

You'll Always Be My Child

Andrea, you're grown and on your own, far away in another state.
We still talk each day on the phone, early morning or very late.
I pray that you live a happy and successful life, without
strife.
I raised you to be as independent as you can, not having to depend on man.
You went to college to achieve a goal in your chosen field.
You made me so happy when you graduated with a skill.
I'm so proud of you for your success, but you'll always be my child nonetheless.

A Lady Named Shirley

There once was a lady named Shirley.
I met her over twenty-five years ago.
She was honored at the Sam Rayburn Center, by folks who loved her so.
Shirley was a person who stood for what was right, expressing fairness without a fight.
I had the honor of shaking her hand.
She was gentle and sweet as any woman on land.
I still have our picture together, to remember that great day.
It was an honor for me to be a part of her fame.
Shirley Chisholm is her full name.
She signed my program, and this made me proud, having something to carry home as my very own.
Shirley stood for women and minorities as a congresswoman of her time.
Serving eight years was a once in a lifetime.
I'll never forget that summer day,
Having lunch with Shirley Chisholm was headway.

Remembering Lisa

Roses are red, violets are blue.
Lisa Fraizer, we will miss you.
You yell real loud when a phone is down,
But pleasantly says "good job" when a sale is made,
Even though some have clowned around.

You often reminded us that the quota for the night was low and then smiled and said,
OK, let's go; you, guys, let's go.
Guys or gals, whatever the case,
You're still the supervisor that
manages to win every race.

You always told us how awesome we were, when we made a lot of sales.
We never heard an unkind word of defeat, not even when most monitors still read 0 complete.

I've only known you five months and a day,
But it seems like I've been here a long time, needless to say.
Just like all the rest, good luck, Liza Fraizer; you're the best.

Katrina and Rita

Being destructive
You have, and then all is gone.
No more, vanished.

What Is Wrong with Our Youth?

Life is being cut short for our youth today.
Have they forgotten what it means to obey?
They are living life at such a fast pace,
Their priorities so out of place.
Children need to be children as long as they can.
There is plenty of time for them to be men.

They must learn to respect the people they affect.
More parental guidance and support are two ways to save our youth.
Community involvement can be our best invaluable sleuth.
Everybody working as a team will make our youth supreme.
They won't have a chance to get in trouble,
If it is recognized, an adult will intervene on the double.

What is wrong with our youth?
Does anyone have the answer?
Good character will tell the whole truth.
This is the only way to save our youth.

My Three Best Friends

I have three best friends.
They are Barbara, Delores, and Ruth.
It seems like we've known each other since youth.
We met over twenty-nine years ago.
Our friendship has become more than just a friendly hello.
We have been best friends a long time,
Many think we are related, because we so gracefully chime.
Our friendship has been one that has become so dear.
In spite of obstacles, we always manage to persevere.
We have had many ladies' night-out events, including
Shopping, eating, bus trips, and our sleepover,
And enjoy the many trips we take to Dover.
We exchange Christmas gifts every year, although we sometimes have to combine three years into one.
There isn't enough time to get everything done.
That's because our schedules get so crammed,
We have to come up with a new program.
I love the fellowship we have acquired
For this measure, we have been admired.
I'm proud of my three best friends.
Preserved friendship with God in control never ends.

Friends

Friends are people who stay by your side through thick and thin.
They are friends to the end.
Whatever they do, they always work together.
They are not people you can only depend on in fair weather.
When one cries, everybody cries.
Helping each other get through a crisis always applies.
Friends talk to each other about any problem without embarrassment.
Just moments in conversation results in time well spent.
Friends respect each other, having an attachment that only love causes to occur.

All I Can Be

I will be all I can be.
I will reach for the top and never stop.
Hold my hand and I'll lead the way.
Come, because I'll be someone special someday.

A Salute to Cynthia Carney

Cynthia, we became Lakeview friends a few years ago.
We always pulled each other up when we were low.
Although your Lakeview stay was short,
You really talked, and you really taught.

True friends are few and far between.
But you're one of the best I've ever seen.
You've served your country and city well.
There are so many stories you could really tell.

Our ages are a few years apart,
But you've been a true friend, and that's from the heart.
God bless you for being honored in a special way.
I'm glad I was invited so I could tell you today.

Press on for more good things to come.
This is an honor that only goes to some.
We crossed paths because of our insights about life,
With our endurance, we always got through the strife.

Good thoughts have been with us all over the world.
Only I know what you mean when you say "Do your thing, girl."
We had some good laughs on hall 2 that bought us to tears.
We needed that laughter to calm our fears.

We knew tomorrow's challenges would keep growing.
However, we managed to do our plans and keep going.
All new situations were faced with a big smile
Cynthia Carney, you're Hodges Manor's teacher of the year, with style.

A Salute to Charles Gibson

Charles Gibson has served his country well,
He always had a story to tell.
Being a part of *Good Morning America* for nineteen years,
His way of telling the news made you listen with both ears.

I know Diane and Robin will miss him in the morning time,
Since his news was so precise and prime.
Although he's leaving the early morning show,
He's set and ready to go.

His steps, on Wednesday, June 28, 2006, will have an extra swing,
This will be when his last bell rings.
When GMA gives him that farewell bash,
It will be like a news flash.

Charles Gibson won't go far, and that's all right.
Just seeing him on *World News Tonight*,
His demeanor will certainly be dynamite.

Why the Southall Family Uses Surf

As clothes are washing,
Surf does the sloshing.
It goes in and out to fight away dirt.
Surf makes each piece of cloth come out just right.

The Southall family uses Surf.
It gives clothes such a fresh smell
It makes those wearing them jump up and yell.
As clothes come out the wash, they look good.

BVG